GEORGINA RODGERS

Foreword by Rachel Kelly

A YEAR of READING ALOUD

52 Poems to Learn and Love

yellow
kite

First published in Great Britain in 2018 by Yellow Kite
An imprint of Hodder & Stoughton
An Hachette UK company

1

Hardback ISBN 978 1 473 6 70891
eBook ISBN 978 1 473 6 70907

Typeset in Arrus BT by Hewer Text UK Ltd, Edinburgh
Printed and bound in Great Britain by Clays Ltd, Elcograf S.p.A.

Yellow Kite
Hodder & Stoughton Ltd
Carmelite House
50 Victoria Embankment
London EC4Y 0DZ

www.yellowkitebooks.co.uk
www.hodder.co.uk

Contents

Foreword

How can learning a poem by heart help us? Let me count the ways.

The first is when I'm feeling wobbly. Even though I'm now recovered, and feel calm and well, in the past I've suffered from debilitating depression. Then poetry proved a friend in need indeed. I wasn't well enough to read anything new. Thank goodness I already had some emergency supplies in the form of a head stocked with a few choice poems, many of them to be found in this stunning anthology.

As I recited poems like Rumi's *The Guest House* in my hospital bed, I felt as if I was having a conversation across the ages. Even though he was writing as a mystic in the thirteenth-century, Rumi created a second voice in my head, a more compassionate, gentle yet firm voice that spoke of forgiveness and understanding. Something good would come of difficult times. I should be 'grateful for whoever comes/Because each has been sent/as a guide from beyond.'

I derived solace from other poems about nature's soothing balm, verse like Mary Oliver's *Wild Geese,* and childhood favourites like *Silver* by Walter de la Mare with its 'Silver fruit upon silver trees', also to be found in this anthology. They calmed me by transporting me to a different place.

Then as I recovered, poems like W. E. Henley's *Invictus* gave me the words needed for the courage and perseverance to keep going. Many was the morning when I mumbled his words as I came downstairs, steadying myself on the bannister. I would repeat to myself 'I am the master of my fate/I am the captain of my soul.' Other poems inspired me when I couldn't sleep. Nothing beats insomnia like repeating lines such as 'Leaving behind nights of terror and fear/I rise/ Into a daybreak that's wondrously clear' from Maya Angelou's empowering paean to rising above hardship *Still, I Rise*.

Second, I turn to the poems I know by heart when I'm bored. Those times when I have forgotten anything to read, and can resist the lure of my phone or it has run out of battery. Waiting in line. Queuing for a bus. The amazing thing about knowing poetry by heart is that you can't lose it. It's part of you, the clue being in the word 'heart'. What those words imply is that what is learnt becomes a part of us, just about as much a part of us as own bodily organs, and scarcely less irreversibly. How brilliant is that. You need never be restless again.

And thirdly, I turn to quoting poems when I'm with friends and family who are searching for something pithy and true and eloquent to make sense of their lives. I seem wittier and wiser by association when I share the words of our literary greats. The poems in this selection will come not just to your rescue but to those you love too, whether they are overpowered by love (*I Carry Your Heart With Me* by E. E. Cummings) or have had a baby (William Blake's *Infant Joy*) or just need to make a fractious child laugh (Edward Lear's *There Was an Old Man with a Beard*).

All of this relies on having memorised the poems ahead so you can whip out the lines when needed. I think of it like having a treasure chest at the ready: Googling a first line isn't half as powerful. So my favourites tend to be short poems, just as they are in this anthology. Partly, brief poems stretch a poet's ability to sum up something to perfection. Secondly,

I prefer to have more shorter poems in my head than fewer, longer ones.

Which brings me to my final point about the virtue of memorising poetry. It's a terrific mental workout for the brain. The more you commit to memory, the easier it becomes, I've found. And it zaps my tendency to worry about the future or regret the past by forcing me to concentrate in the moment as I learn my lines.

Now, thanks to *A Year of Reading Aloud* the process will become easier still. Here is a selection of short, brilliant poems for almost every eventuality with masterful introductions which elucidate both poem and poet, one for each week of the year.

There's plenty of old friends, and some new discoveries such as the work of the younger generation and their musings on feminism, love and self-awareness, poems such as *All or Nothing* by Lang Leav and *there will always be your heart* by Yrsa Daley-Ward. Each and every poem deserves to be learnt by heart. Poetry can prove the thing for hope, perching in your soul.

Rachel Kelly
London, June 2018

Introduction

*'Poetry can tell us what human beings are.
It can tell us why we stumble and fall and how,
miraculously, we can stand up.'*
MAYA ANGELOU

We all spend a lot of time trying to look after and nurture ourselves; from booking luxurious holidays and digital detox retreats, through to following the latest eating plans or fitness fads that promise improved health and vitality. However, when was the last time you sat down and really studied a poem? You may never have considered that learning poems and reciting them aloud should be added to your list of go-to wellness treatments, and you might be surprised to learn that such an activity brings not just huge pleasure, but health and well-being benefits too.

We all grow up with a deep and intrinsic love of words and poetry. As babies and children, rhyme and rhythm have a natural place in our lives, with gentle lullabies, bouncy nursery rhymes and playground choruses. Small children may not understand the words of these rhymes but they delight in the melodies and sounds. As we learn the words, we can feel them as they form in our mouths and our bodies naturally dance to the rhythms. At school, we learn about important poets and study their work, memorise verses and recite them until the words are permanently etched in our minds. Some poems are woven so deeply into the architecture of our lives and our culture that they inform our understanding of the world.

The power of poetry lies in its ability to evoke emotions, thoughts and memories in only a few words. There is no set of rules when it comes to reading poetry; its timeless melodies and phrases are open to interpretation. Poetry can, through a simple verse, speak to us more coherently and meaningfully than a close friend or relative. Poems bring with them solace, bravery, passion, beauty, kindness, sympathy, and even the ugliest of emotions are transformed into something more precise and graceful. Sometimes it's as if poems don't even register with our brains and therefore logic and reason; they bypass them to speak immediately to our hearts or souls. The joy of a poem is how, as readers, we can delicately place ourselves into the words and along the poem's path or journey, reading our own experiences, struggles or triumphs in its narrative. It allows us to face the world with a new understanding, perspective or reason. We can take poetry with us as something to hold on to. Even more than that, each time we read a certain poem, we can find new meanings, colour and layers in its words, as if we are reading it for the first time.

The oral tradition and the benefits of memorisation

While poetry as we know it is in a written form, it derives from a singing and oral speaking tradition. Reciting poetry is as old as time, and poems are written to be read out loud, with pace, musicality and emotion measured by the poem's meter, or pattern of stressed and unstressed syllables. Before the invention of writing, the only way to pass on stories, poems or fables from one generation to another was through memorising and reciting them. Ancient Greeks used recitation for awakening the mind and shaping character. They made poetry the foundation of their teaching methods, and at social gatherings people recited stories of their history and tales of Ancient Greek gods and goddesses in long, rhymed narratives. Later, memorising poetry was also once a tool used to improve people's memories in order to better their knowledge of the bible and to gain a heightened feel for language. During Shakespeare's time, it is said that it was common for people to learn large swathes of text.

By the beginning of the 19th century, reciting poetry in class was seen as important because it improved delivery and elocution. As time wore on, benefits such as self-discipline, physical awareness and posture were all added to the mix. Memorising poetry at school is now seen as an important tool to stretch cognitive development, reading comprehension and language capability. However, as adults, memorisation is of deeper value than ever before. In an age when all we need is a couple of search terms to type into Google, depth of learning and memorisation have been replaced with learning how to skim, where there is so much information, content and reading material that even the most compelling barely leaves an imprint on our consciousness. We now live in a world where many of us almost solely exist within a social media bubble; platforms like Facebook, Instagram and Twitter become our go-to place for content, words and information.

Mindfulness, of whatever kind, calls us back to focus on where we are and to observe that moment in time, so there is little space for unbidden thoughts. To concentrate on any poem hard enough to memorise it, we must pay attention to each word, line and stanza, just as the poet did as they wrote it. As US poet Muriel Rukeyser once said: 'This moment is real, this moment is what we have, this moment in which we face each other, and if a poem is any damn good at all, it invites you to bring your whole life to that moment, and we are good poets inasmuch as we bring that invitation to you, and you are good readers inasmuch as you bring your whole life to the reading of the poem.'

In a world where life moves at a breakneck speed, by taking time to read a poem and recite it, you are forced to slow down. In order to really learn a poem, you need to chew the words over and over. Poetry is the opposite of instant – it makes us take a deep breath and really take time to understand what we are reading. Some meanings aren't immediately clear, and are more opaque and harder to grasp, but the important thing is what a poem means to us and how it makes us feel.

Memorising poetry exercises the brain and gives it strength to learn and remember other information: it's a case of the more we learn, the more we learn. And in the same way having a good working memory is good for learning, it is also good for creativity, focus and problem-solving. This type of learning through memorisation strengthens neuroplasticity – the 'muscle-building' part of the brain, and studies show that older people who engage in intensive periods of it have improved memory and verbal recall overall, as well as delayed cognitive decline.

The poetry challenge and memorisation tips

A Year of Reading Aloud includes some of the best-loved poems of the past, alongside newer poetry, including a handful of verses from Instapoets like Yrsa Daley-Ward and

Nikita Gill. The challenge is to learn one poem every week for a year. It is not necessary to start at the beginning of this book and work your way through; simply find a poem that resonates with you that week, learn it off by heart and recite it to family, friends or anyone else who will listen! Do not allow yourself to be intimidated by poetry or put off by memories of strict teachers and stuffy exam halls. Be inspired, learn new viewpoints, surprise yourself. The subject matter of these poems varies widely, but having a wide range of poetry stored in your memory can be a powerful tool and lead to improved psychological and intellectual well-being.

So how do you memorise a poem? There are many opinions about the best way to do this and everyone will find something that works best for them.

Here are some ideas:

🌸 Choose a poem that you like: the more you connect with a poem, the more likely you are to be able to learn it off by heart. It's like music; the songs we find ourselves singing are the ones that resonate with us. Find the poems that make you feel deeply.

🌸 Take your time to get to know and understand the poem: read it aloud a few times, write it out a number of times, look up words you do not understand and make sure you recognise the meter.

🌸 Build a storyline: try to make connections between verses or stanzas by creating a storyline or outline in your mind. Numerous studies have shown that our memories work better when we create vivid stories when we are learning.

❊ Take one or two lines at a time: use opportunities such as walking, commuting or eating your breakfast to learn a line or two. When you memorise a new line, recite the whole poem from the beginning.

❊ Repeat, repeat, repeat: the best way to learn anything is to expose yourself to it as much as possible, so keep repeating it.

❊ Test yourself: once you think you have learnt the whole poem, recite it frequently when it isn't to hand.

❊ Recite: one of the greatest joys of memorising poetry is being able to recite it to others. Whether it's to your children around the breakfast table, your colleagues at work or amongst a group of friends, challenge yourself to recite your poem clearly and passionately, and remember to project your voice. Next time you throw a party, recite some poetry. Relax and enjoy yourself!

'Hope' is the Thing with Feathers

EMILY DICKINSON (1830–1886)

Emily Dickinson is considered one of America's finest and most original poets. Challenging the definition of poetry itself and a poet's work, she played with form and expression, creating a unique and dynamic voice. She wrote over 1,800 poems, although only seven were published while she was still alive. When the first volume of her poetry was published in 1890, it was met with huge critical acclaim and success. During the early 1860s, Dickinson is said to have suffered an emotional crisis, inspiring her to write extensively, and in 1862 when she wrote this poem, she is said to have composed 300 poems, offering insights into mortality, fame and the soul.

'Hope' is the Thing with Feathers is an extended metaphor, likening the concept of hope to a small bird, who is perched on the soul of each of us, singing in its quest to inspire. Life-affirming, this sparkling poem transcends the test of time, suggesting that even during the most difficult of times, hope can sustain us.

'Hope' is the thing with feathers –
That perches in the soul –
And sings the tune without the words –
And never stops – at all –

And sweetest – in the Gale – is heard –
And sore must be the storm –
That could abash the little Bird
That kept so many warm –

I've heard it in the chillest land –
And on the strangest Sea –
Yet – never – in Extremity,
It asked a crumb – of me.

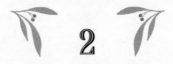

2

The Guest House

RUMI (1207–1273)

The poems of Jalal ad-Din Muhammad Rumi, a Persian poet and Sufi master, have millions of devoted followers around the world. He is often described as the bestselling poet in the United States and his legion of fans includes Beyoncé and Jay-Z – who named their twin daughter, born in June 2017, after him – and Chris Martin, who said that Rumi's poetry changed his life. Rumi is considered a captivating figure throughout many countries and cultures and his work has an embracing universality, crossing different times, places and religions.

The Guest House speaks of the human condition, where he tells us that every experience and emotion we have is a valuable one. The poem is frequently recited at mindfulness and meditation programmes across the globe, and encourages us to embrace the uncertainty of life.

This being human is a guest house.
Every morning a new arrival.

A joy, a depression, a meanness,
some momentary awareness comes
as an unexpected visitor.

Welcome and entertain them all!
Even if they're a crowd of sorrows,
who violently sweep your house
empty of its furniture,
still, treat every guest honourably.
He may be clearing you out
For some new delight.

The dark thought, the shame, the malice,
Meet them at the door laughing,
and invite them in.

Be grateful for whoever comes,
Because each has been sent
as a guide from beyond.

3

Piano

D. H. LAWRENCE (1885–1930)

English novelist, playwright, literary critic and poet D. H. Lawrence is regarded as one of the most influential writers of the 20th century and a voice of modernism. He is perhaps best known for his controversial works, including the infamous novel *Lady Chatterley's Lover*, which was banned in Britain until 1960. He spent much of his life in voluntary exile; a time he called his 'savage pilgrimage'.

Piano was first published in 1918 and is about childhood memories that are triggered by beautiful music. The speaker talks about a simpler time and a longing to return to the past.

Softly, in the dusk, a woman is singing to me;
Taking me back down the vista of years, till I see
A child sitting under the piano, in the boom of the
    tingling strings
And pressing the small, poised feet of a mother who
    smiles as she sings.

In spite of myself, the insidious mastery of song
Betrays me back, till the heart of me weeps to belong
To the old Sunday evenings at home, with winter
    outside
And hymns in the cosy parlour, the tinkling piano our
    guide.

So now it is vain for the singer to burst into clamour
With the great black piano appassionato. The glamour
Of childish days is upon me, my manhood is cast
Down in the flood of remembrance, I weep like a child
    for the past.

I Carry Your Heart With Me

E. E. CUMMINGS (1894–1962)

Edward Estlin Cummings – often styled as e.e. cummings – was an American poet, playwright, painter, author and essayist. He was passionate about poetry as a child, writing one poem a day between the ages of eight and twenty-two. He experimented with poetic form, punctuation and language, creating a unique, bold voice and signature style known for its lack of conformity, forgoing capitalisation and punctuation, breaking words up and interjecting syllables of other words between them. His poetry was both loved and hated by his contemporaries and critics.

Many of his poems focus on love and nature, and *I Carry Your Heart With Me*, first published in 1952, is about the unbreakable and overpowering force of love. This is one of his most popular poems, and is a favourite at weddings.

i carry your heart with me (i carry it in
my heart) i am never without it (anywhere
i go you go, my dear; and whatever is done
by only me is your doing, my darling)

                                  i fear
no fate (for you are my fate, my sweet) i want
no world (for beautiful you are my world, my true)
and it's you are whatever a moon has always meant
and whatever a sun will always sing is you

here is the deepest secret nobody knows
(here is the root of the root and the bud of the bud
and the sky of the sky of a tree called life; which grows
higher than soul can hope or mind can hide)
and this is the wonder that's keeping the stars apart

i carry your heart (i carry it in my heart)

5

Dreams

LANGSTON HUGHES (1902–1967)

James Mercer Langston Hughes was an African-American poet, activist, playwright and novelist, who was first recognised for his literary efforts during the 1920s. This period, where a number of black artists created a new cultural identity through their work, was called the 'Harlem Renaissance'. As one of the leaders of this artistic explosion, Hughes' work was recognised for its lucidity, simplicity of style and the voice he gave to everyday men and women.

Hughes wrote this poem at a time when racism meant that black people's dreams were silenced, but the message holds true across cultures and time; we all must have ambition, dreams and goals to give our lives purpose and meaning.

Hold fast to dreams
For if dreams die
Life is a broken-winged bird
That cannot fly.

Hold fast to dreams
For when dreams go
Life is a barren field
Frozen with snow.

6

There Was an Old Man with a Beard

EDWARD LEAR (1812–1888)

Along with Lewis Carroll, English author, writer and artist Edward Lear was known for writing 'nonsense verse', a form of writing that depicts imaginative or absurd characters using meaningless or 'nonsense' words. He is perhaps best known for his whimsical poem, *The Owl and the Pussycat*. One of his most famous inventions, the 'runcible spoon', is now found in many English dictionaries. He had begun to write a sequel, *The Children of the Owl and the Pussycat*, but sections of the poem remained incomplete at the time of his death.

He was also a pioneer of the limerick – a five-line comic verse – and helped to popularise it in his 1846 book, *The Book of Nonsense*. The popularity of this book, which Lear illustrated himself, was a landmark in the acceptance of nonsense writing for children.

There was an Old Man with a beard,
Who said, 'It is just as I feared!–
Two Owls and a Hen,
Four Larks and a Wren,
Have all built their nests in my beard.'

In the Forest

OSCAR WILDE (1854–1900)

Much of the poetry of Irish playwright and poet Oscar Wilde is overshadowed by his fictional works, and his lasting literary fame lies with plays, including *Lady Windermere's Fan* and *The Importance of Being Earnest*, and his only novel, *The Picture of Dorian Gray*. An iconic figure in Victorian society, he was renowned for his flamboyant and eccentric style and cutting wit. The most enduring of his poems is *The Ballad of Reading Gaol*, a verse he wrote after being imprisoned when he was found guilty of homosexuality. He was forced to do hard labour and contracted meningitis, which ultimately led to his demise.

This short poem, first published in the *Lady's Pictorial* in 1889, celebrates the elusive and fleeting nature of love and the thrill of the chase.

Out of the mid-wood's twilight
Into the meadow's dawn,
Ivory limbed and brown-eyed,
Flashes my Faun!

He skips through the copses singing,
And his shadow dances along,
And I know not which I should follow,
Shadow or song!

O Hunter, snare me his shadow!
O Nightingale, catch me his strain!
Else moonstruck with music and madness
I track him in vain!

Now Winter Nights Enlarge

THOMAS CAMPION (1567–1620)

The poetry of Thomas Campion is known for its lyrical quality and mastery of rhythmic structure, because the writer was also a composer and brilliant lutenist. A true 'Renaissance man', Campion was very popular in courtly circles and wrote masques for royals and nobles. He was also a doctor by profession.

Published in the *Third and Fourth Books of Ayres* in 1617, *Now Winter Nights Enlarge* explores the delights of the long winter nights that seem short because of the enjoyable ways they have been spent. It is worth noting that this verse was originally written to be accompanied to music.

Now winter nights enlarge
The number of their hours
And clouds their storms discharge
Upon the airy towers.
Let now the chimneys blaze
And cups o'erflow with wine:
Let well-tun'd words amaze
With harmony divine.
Now yellow waxen lights
Shall wait on honey love
While youthful Revels, Masques, and Courtly sights
Sleep's leaden spells remove.

This time doth well dispense
With lovers' long discourse;
Much speech hath some defence,
Though beauty no remorse.
All do not all things well;
Some measures comely tread,
Some knotted Riddles tell,
Some poems smoothly read.
The Summer hath his joys,
And Winter his delights;
Though Love and all his pleasures are but toys,
They shorten tedious nights.

A Dream Within A Dream

EDGAR ALLAN POE (1809-1849)

A Dream Within a Dream

EDGAR ALLAN POE (1809–1849)

During his short literary career, American writer, editor and literary critic Edgar Allan Poe produced a large body of poetry and short stories that captured the imaginations and hearts of his readers. He is most famous for his tales of the macabre and he is said to have completely transformed the genre of the horror story.

A Dream Within a Dream, a mature poem that he wrote in his later years, questions human existence and the nature of reality, and looks at whether fundamental perceptions are not what they seem. In 1849, he wrote in the periodical the *Southern Literary Messenger*: 'It is by no means an irrational fancy that, in future existence, we shall look upon what we think our present existence, as a dream.'

This poem is based on an earlier work, *Imitation*, published in 1827, which tackles similar ideas about the mystery of life.

Take this kiss upon the brow!
And, in parting from you now,
Thus much let me avow –
You are not wrong, who deem
That my days have been a dream;
Yet if hope has flown away
In a night, or in a day,
In a vision, or in none,
Is it therefore the less gone?
All that we see or seem
Is but a dream within a dream.

I stand amid the roar
Of a surf-tormented shore,
And I hold within my hand
Grains of the golden sand –
How few! yet how they creep
Through my fingers to the deep,
While I weep – while I weep!
O God! can I not grasp
Them with a tighter clasp?
O God! can I not save
One from the pitiless wave?
Is all that we see or seem
But a dream within a dream?

10

Upon Westminster Bridge

WILLIAM WORDSWORTH (1770–1850)

William Wordsworth was one of the major poets of the Romantic movement in Britain, whose poems often focused on the landscapes of the Lake District, including the world of nature and the people who lived and worked there. This poem is unusual because he takes London as his subject, describing the splendour and beauty of the city, viewed from Westminster Bridge early in the morning.

First published in the collection *Poems, in Two Volumes* in 1807, this stately sonnet was said to have been written when Wordsworth was travelling in 1802 with his sister, Dorothy, to Calais in France, and they crossed the bridge to get out of town on the roof of the coach (he could not afford to travel inside it). He was en route to meet his illegitimate daughter, Caroline – born to his former French mistress, Annette Vallon, in 1792 – for the first time.

Earth has not anything to show more fair:
Dull would he be of soul who could pass by
A sight so touching in its majesty:
This City now doth, like a garment, wear

The beauty of the morning: silent, bare,
Ships, towers, domes, theatres, and temples lie
Open unto the fields, and to the sky;
All bright and glittering in the smokeless air.

Never did sun more beautifully steep
In his first splendour, valley, rock, or hill;
Ne'er saw I, never felt, a calm so deep!

The river glideth at his own sweet will:
Dear God! the very houses seem asleep;
And all that mighty heart is lying still!

11

Leisure

W. H. DAVIES (1871–1940)

William Henry Davies, who wrote as W. H. Davies, was a Welsh poet and writer. He spent some time homeless, riding the freight trains of America and in hostels in London – sometimes begging in order to survive – before finding literary success. He later documented his life in his acclaimed memoir, *Autobiography of a Super-Tramp*.

His work often explores themes of hardship, city life and the natural world. *Leisure* first appeared in *Songs of Joy and Others* in 1911 and was published again in his first anthology, *Collected Poems*, in 1916.

Leisure suggests that the hectic pace of life has a detrimental effect on the human spirit, and we all need to live our lives 'free from care' and spend more time appreciating nature around us. This message is perhaps even more relevant today, with the effects of technology, than it was at the time of writing.

What is this life if, full of care,
We have no time to stand and stare.
No time to stand beneath the boughs
And stare as long as sheep and cows.
No time to see, when woods we pass,
Where squirrels hide their nuts in grass.
No time to see, in broad daylight,
Streams full of stars, like skies at night.
No time to turn at Beauty's glance,
And watch her feet, how they can dance.
No time to wait till her mouth can
Enrich that smile her eyes began?
A poor life this if, full of care,
We have no time to stand and stare.

12

Thinking

WALTER D. WINTLE

Unfortunately, almost nothing is known about Wintle himself, except that he lived in the late 19th and early 20th centuries. There has been some speculation that his name may have been a pseudonym for a more well-known writer.

Thinking – also known as *The Man Who Thinks He Can* – is said to have been published for the first time in 1905, and a number of different versions exist. The poem is a helpful reminder of the amount of power and influence positive thinking can have.

If you think you are beaten, you are.
If you think you dare not, you don't.
If you like to win, but think you can't,
It's a cinch you won't.

If you think you'll lose, you're lost
For out of the world we find
Success begins with a fellow's will.
It's all in a state of mind.

If you think you are outclassed, you are.
You've got to think high to rise.
You've got to be sure of yourself before
You can ever win a prize.

Life's battles don't always go
To the stronger or faster man.
But sooner or later the man who wins
Is the man who thinks he can.

13

The Eagle

ALFRED, LORD TENNYSON (1809–1892)

Widely considered to be one of the most influential British figures in literature during the Victorian era, Alfred, Lord Tennyson first began writing poetry as a young boy and, at the age of twelve, he wrote a poem that was 6,000 lines long. Many of his works are much revered and loved, among them *In Memoriam A.H.H.*, which contains the line, ''Tis better to have loved and lost, than never to have loved at all.'

The Eagle, a short and punchy poem, was written in the 1830s before Tennyson was recognised as one of the best poets of his era. He is said to have been inspired to write this verse during his travels in the Pyrenees, where he wrote about a valley that he later described as his favourite place in the world. The freedom and beauty of the bird of prey are captured in this short verse.

Tennyson was appointed Poet Laureate in 1850, a year before *The Eagle* was published. He held this position until his death; the longest time that anyone has held the post.

He clasps the crag with crooked hands;
Close to the sun in lonely lands,
Ringed with the azure world, he stands.

The wrinkled sea beneath him crawls;
He watches from his mountain walls,
And like a thunderbolt he falls.

He Wishes for the Cloths of Heaven

W. B. YEATS (1865–1939)

William Butler Yeats, whose work was influenced by the politics and heritage of Ireland, is widely considered one of the greatest poets of the English language, and in 1923 he won the Nobel Prize for Literature.

This poem is one of his most popular verses, and his shortest. Published in 1899 in his third volume of poetry *The Wind Among the Reeds*, it appeared under the title, *Aedh Wishes for the Cloths of Heaven*, Aedh being the speaker, who was later retitled with the more generic 'he'.

Simple in structure and using powerful and luxurious imagery, the pale and lovesick speaker fantasises about being able to buy cloths worthy of heavenly light, and placing them under the feet of his lover. An interesting and intense take on unrequited love, Yeats is said to have written this for Maud Gonne, an Irish revolutionary and suffragette he loved for most of his life, but who did not return his feelings.

Had I the heaven's embroidered cloths,
Enwrought with golden and silver light,
The blue and the dim and the dark cloths
Of night and light and the half-light,
I would spread the cloths under your feet:
But I, being poor, have only my dreams;
I have spread my dreams under your feet;
Tread softly because you tread on my dreams.

15

Wild Geese

MARY OLIVER (BORN 1935)

Pulitzer Prize-winning American writer Mary Oliver is known for her writing about a profound connection to the natural world, and her work is often compared to that of Emily Dickinson, with whom she shares a love of solitude and introspection. She published her first collection of poetry, *No Voyage and Other Poems*, in 1963 and has since become one of the most beloved poets of her generation, winning many prizes for her work.

Wild Geese first appeared in her 1986 anthology *Dream Work* and it provided the title of her 2004 collection of poems. This poem is about what we must do to lead a good life, by being true to nature and its beauty.

You do not have to be good.
You do not have to walk on your knees
for a hundred miles through the desert, repenting.
You only have to let the soft animal of your body
love what it loves.
Tell me about despair, yours, and I will tell you mine.
Meanwhile the world goes on.
Meanwhile the sun and the clear pebbles of the rain
are moving across the landscapes,
over the prairies and the deep trees,
the mountains and the rivers.
Meanwhile the wild geese, high in the clean blue air,
are heading home again.
Whoever you are, no matter how lonely,
the world offers itself to your imagination,
calls to you like the wild geese, harsh and exciting –
over and over announcing your place
in the family of things.

16

Infant Joy

WILLIAM BLAKE (1757–1827)

The work of visionary and expressive British poet William Blake was largely unrecognised during his lifetime, but he is now considered a seminal figure in the history of British art and literature. Blake's writing is said to have influenced and inspired countless writers and artists throughout the ages. During his lifetime, his main profession was engraving and his favourite pastime was painting with watercolours, although today he is more famous for his poetry.

All his work was coloured by intense spirituality and he is said to have had visions of God from as young as age four, when he saw God 'put his head on the window'. As a result of this, many considered him to be insane.

Infant Joy, focusing on the gift of newborn life and innocence, was first published as part of his collection *Songs of Innocence* in 1789. This poem is a counterpart to *Infant Sorrow*, which was published in his later collection *Songs of Experience* in 1794, which also featured his famous poem, *The Tyger*.

I have no name.
I am but two days old.
What shall I call thee?
'I happy am,
Joy is my name.
Sweet joy befall thee!

Pretty joy!
Sweet joy but two days old.
Sweet joy I call thee;
Thou dost smile.
I sing the while
Sweet joy befall thee!

17

Invictus

W. E. HENLEY (1849–1903)

William Ernest Henley was an influential British poet, best known for this poem which he wrote in 1875 and published in 1888 in his first volume of poems, *Book of Verses*. 'Invictus' is the Latin word for 'unconquerable' and Henley composed this verse during a long spell in hospital, where he was being treated for tuberculosis of the bone, also known as Pott's disease. He had contracted the disease aged twelve and had lost one of his legs below the knee in his twenties. He feared he would lose the other leg but he enlisted the help of Dr Joseph Lister, a surgeon and pioneer of antiseptic surgery. Henley's leg was saved, and during his twenty-month stay at the Royal Edinburgh Infirmary, he wrote *Invictus* along with a handful of other poems.

This inspiring, bold and powerful poem was said to be a favourite with Nelson Mandela, who recited it to other prisoners during the twenty-seven years that he was incarcerated, as a way to bolster their spirits. It is a poignant reminder that we are in charge of our own destinies.

Out of the night that covers me,
Black as the pit from pole to pole.
I thank whatever gods may be
For my unconquerable soul.

In the fell clutch of circumstance,
I have not winced nor cried aloud.
Under the bludgeonings of chance
My head is bloody, but unbowed.

Beyond this place of wrath and tears,
Looms but the Horror of the shade,
And yet the menace of the years
Finds, and shall find, me unafraid.

It matters not how strait the gate,
How charged with punishments the scroll,
I am the master of my fate:
I am the captain of my soul.

18

Trees

JOYCE KILMER (1886–1918)

This lyrical poem by young American writer Alfred Joyce Kilmer is regarded as his most famous, and thought to be one of the most quoted poems in American history. Written in February 1913 and first published in *Poetry: A Magazine in Verse* the following August, it was included in his 1914 collection *Trees and Other Poems*, where it quickly gained attention.

The poem showcases the speaker's connection with nature and its beauty, giving trees human emotions and attributes, and it has been enjoyed by generations for its simplicity. Many critics have speculated about where the poem was written, but according to Kilmer's oldest son, Kenton, he wrote it while sitting in an upstairs room at the family home in Mahwah, New Jersey, looking down on the garden, and he intended the poem to be about all different types of trees.

Kilmer was a decorated war hero and was tragically killed in France during World War I, aged thirty-one, just five years after *Trees* won him national acclaim.

I think that I shall never see
A poem lovely as a tree.

A tree whose hungry mouth is prest
Against the earth's sweet flowing breast;

A tree that looks at God all day,
And lifts her leafy arms to pray;

A tree that may in Summer wear
A nest of robins in her hair;

Upon whose bosom snow has lain;
Who intimately lives with rain.

Poems are made by fools like me,
But only God can make a tree.

19

Echo

CHRISTINA ROSSETTI (1830–1894)

One of the most important British writers of the 19th century, Christina Rossetti is best known for her fantastical works, religious poems and verses for children. Her Christmas poem, *In the Bleak Midwinter*, became widely known after her death when it was set to music.

Born into a family of scholars and writers, Rossetti had her first book of poetry privately printed, aged twelve, by her grandfather. As the sister of painter-poet Dante Gabriel Rossetti, she was at the centre of the Pre-Raphaelite movement in the mid–late Victorian period, a group which challenged conventions in art. A major influence in her work was her religious belief.

She composed *Echo* in 1854 and it was first published in *Goblin Market and Other Poems* in 1862, which received widespread critical acclaim. This melancholic lyric poem is a beautiful expression of grief and longing to find a loved one after they have died.

Come to me in the silence of the night;
Come in the speaking silence of a dream;
Come with soft rounded cheeks and eyes as bright
As sunlight on a stream;
Come back in tears,
O memory, hope and love of finished years.

O dream how sweet, too sweet, too bitter sweet,
Whose wakening should have been in Paradise,
Where souls brimfull of love abide and meet;
Where thirsting longing eyes
Watch the slow door
That opening, letting in, lets out no more.

Yet come to me in dreams, that I may live
My very life again tho' cold in death:
Come back to me in dreams, that I may give
Pulse for pulse, breath for breath:
Speak low, lean low,
As long ago, my love, how long ago.

20

The Old Pond

BASHO MATSUO (1644–1694)

The tradition of writing haiku, or Japanese short poetry, first started with Buddhist monks in Japan and then spread throughout the world. A haiku consists of just three lines and seventeen syllables, with five syllables on the first line, seven on the next and five on the third (although this structure is often impossible to replicate in translation, as for this example here). The form relies on simple phrases that often capture images in nature.

Basho Matsuo is considered the first great haiku poet and *The Old Pond* is his most famous example; it has been translated a vast number of times. According to legend, he is said to have written it when his Zen master Boncho visited him and asked him a *koan* – a question or riddle without an answer – designed to abandon logical reason to provoke enlightenment. The stillness of the pond is said to represent peace and a kinship with nature and, as the frog jumps in, there is a moment of enlightenment.

Breaking the silence,
Of an ancient pond,
A frog – jumped into water –
A deep resonance.

21

Proud Maisie

WALTER SCOTT (1771–1832)

Even though his first love and success were through writing poetry, Sir Walter Scott's literary reputation now lies in his collection of novels, including his towering group of *Waverley Novels*. During his lifetime, he was considered the most popular author the world had known. His influences are said to include classical myths and legends and his Scottish homeland. It is a measure of his success that Edinburgh's central railway station, opened in 1854, is called Waverley station.

Proud Maisie was published in 1818 in *The Heart of Mid-Lothian*, the seventh of the *Waverley Novels*, and is regarded as one of his best verse compositions. Set in an almost magical woodland, the short and sweet ballad takes the dialogue between Maisie and a 'sweet robin'. Maisie expects the best in life, asking the robin about her wedding, but the bird only foretells a dark future or death.

Proud Maisie is in the wood,
Walking so early;
Sweet Robin sits on the bush,
Singing so rarely.

'Tell me, thou bonny bird,
When shall I marry me?' –
'When six braw gentlemen
Kirkward shall carry ye.'

'Who makes the bridal bed,
Birdie, say truly?' –
'The grey-headed sexton
That delves the grave duly.

'The glowworm o'er grave and stone
Shall light thee steady;
The owl from the steeple sing,
"Welcome proud lady."'

22

Cradle Song

THOMAS DEKKER (1572–1632)

This beautiful lullaby was written by English dramatist and pamphleteer Thomas Dekker as part of the play *Patient Grissel*, co-authored by Henry Chettle and William Haughton. The play, which was first published in 1603, is a take on the medieval tale of Griselda, the patient wife.

The poem was originally set to music in 1918 and, later, Paul McCartney is said to have seen the sheet music at his father's home left on the piano by his step-sister. Inspired by the words but being unable to read the music, he created his own melody and wrote the Beatles song, *Golden Slumbers*, making minor word changes.

Golden slumbers kiss your eyes,
Smiles awake you when you rise;
Sleep, pretty wantons, do not cry,
And I will sing a lullaby,
Rock them, rock them, lullaby.

Care is heavy, therefore sleep you,
You are care, and care must keep you;
Sleep, pretty wantons, do not cry,
And I will sing a lullaby,
Rock them, rock them, lullaby.

23

Sonnet 116

WILLIAM SHAKESPEARE (1564–1616)

Although we now think of him as primarily a playwright, during his own lifetime William Shakespeare was also well known as a poet; he wrote 154 sonnets, likely to have been composed over an extended period of time from 1592–1598. Focusing on the nature of love and beauty, in relationships and relation to time, the sonnets were first published together in 1609, along with his long poem, *The Passionate Pilgrim*. His sonnets, which were considered a form of private expression – with some critics saying Shakespeare never intended them to be published – remain some of the most important written in the English language.

This is one of Shakespeare's most famous love sonnets and is regarded as one of the finest love poems ever written. The poem is a rumination on love and how the love will not be changed, impeded or stopped by circumstances, the passing of time or the fading of youth.

Let me not to the marriage of true minds
Admit impediments. Love is not love
Which alters when it alteration finds,
Or bends with the remover to remove.
O no; it is an ever-fixed mark
That looks on tempests, and is never shaken;
It is the star to every wandering bark,
Whose worth's unknown, although his height be taken.
Love's not Time's fool, though rosy lips and cheeks
Within his bending sickle's compass come;
Love alters not with his brief hours and weeks,
But bears it out even to the edge of doom.
If this be error and upon me proved,
I never writ, nor no man ever loved.

Temporary and Permanent

NIKITA GILL (BORN 1987)

This London-based poet and visual artist had 137 rejection letters from traditional publishers before she began to share her work more widely on Instagram, Tumblr and other online platforms. She started writing poetry as a way of coping with a world that overwhelmed her. She explains: 'Writing was cathartic in a way that helped me breathe again, without relying on other people to help me feel better.' Her work covers topics like empowerment, femininity, identity, love and loss.

Temporary and Permanent explores themes of relationships and loss. She says: 'I've lost so many people in my life and as a sensitive person it hurts me on levels I cannot begin to explain. I wrote this poem to aid my own healing.'

Most people in your life
were only meant
for dreams,
and summer laughter.

They stay till the wind changes,
the tides turn,
or disappear
with the first snow.

And then there are some
that were forged
to weather blizzards
and pain with you.

They were cast in iron,
set in gold
and never ever leave you
to face anything alone.

Know who those people are.
And love them the way they deserve.
Not everyone in your life is temporary.
A few are as permanent as love is old.

25

My Shadow

ROBERT LOUIS STEVENSON (1850–1894)

Robert Louis Stevenson was a Scottish novelist and poet who established his name in the literary world with *Treasure Island*, published in 1883. This poem appeared in 1885 in a collection entitled *Penny Whistles* (better known today as *A Child's Garden of Verses*) along with other classics, such as *The Swing* and *The Lamplighter*.

Written from the perspective of a small child, the speaker cannot understand the true nature of his shadow and why it behaves in such a strange way. It encourages the reader to look at the world with the innocence of a child.

I have a little shadow that goes in and out with me,
And what can be the use of him is more than I can see.
He is very, very like me from the heels up to the head;
And I see him jump before me, when I jump into my
    bed.

The funniest thing about him is the way he likes to
    grow –
Not at all like proper children, which is always very
    slow;
For he sometimes shoots up taller like an india-rubber
    ball,
And he sometimes gets so little that there's none of him
    at all.

He hasn't got a notion of how children ought to play,
And can only make a fool of me in every sort of way.
He stays so close beside me, he's a coward you can see;
I'd think shame to stick to nursie as that shadow sticks
    to me!

One morning, very early, before the sun was up,
I rose and found the shining dew on every buttercup;
But my lazy little shadow, like an arrant sleepy-head,
Had stayed at home behind me and was fast asleep in
    bed.

26

Where the Mind is Without Fear

RABINDRANATH TAGORE (1861–1941)

A native of Calcutta, Rabindranath Tagore is sometimes described as India's equivalent of William Shakespeare. He penned fiction, essays, drama, songs and poetry and, later in his life, turned to art.

The original Bengali language poem *Chitto Jetha Bhayshunyo (Where the Mind is Without Fear)* was published in 1910 and included in the collection *Gitanjali (Song Offerings)*, before India's independence. In 1912, he sailed from India to England with a collection of English translations of around 100 poems within the anthology, and lost the manuscript on the London Tube. Fortunately, he later found it at the Lost Luggage office. In 1913, he became the first non-European to win the Nobel Prize for Literature.

Tagore had deep religious roots and in this poem he paints a moving picture of the country he would have liked India to be; a place in which its people can be at peace and prosper.

Where the mind is without fear and the head is held
  high;
Where knowledge is free;
Where the world has not been broken up into fragments
By narrow domestic walls;
Where words come out from the depth of truth;
Where tireless striving stretches its arms towards
  perfection;
Where the clear stream of reason has not lost its way
Into the dreary desert sand of dead habit;
Where the mind is led forward by thee
Into ever-widening thought and action –
Into that heaven of freedom, my Father, let my country
  awake.

27

The Tide Rises, the Tide Falls

HENRY WADSWORTH LONGFELLOW (1807–1882)

Henry Wadsworth Longfellow is one of the 'Fireside Poets', a group of American poets from New England, who were the first to rival the popularity of British poets, both at home and abroad. Longfellow's poems became mainstays of national culture and school curricula and were regularly read around the fireside in family homes.

Longfellow was a scholar, linguist, traveller and romantic, who identified closely with English literature and thinking. He is one of the few American writers honoured in Poets' Corner at Westminster Abbey.

In 1879, towards the end of his life, Longfellow wrote *The Tide Rises, the Tide Falls;* a poem that is now one of his most famous. He had already witnessed the deaths of his two wives, which had left him heartbroken. Symbolically, this poem is usually seen as talking about human mortality, represented by darkness and the effacement of the traveller's footprints.

The tide rises, the tide falls,
The twilight darkens, the curlew calls;
Along the sea-sands damp and brown
The traveller hastens toward the town,
And the tide rises, the tide falls.

Darkness settles on roofs and walls,
But the sea, the sea in the darkness calls;
The little waves, with their soft, white hands,
Efface the footprints in the sands,
And the tide rises, the tide falls.

The morning breaks; the steeds in their stalls
Stamp and neigh, as the hostler calls;
The day returns, but nevermore
Returns the traveller to the shore,
And the tide rises, the tide falls.

28

The Orange

WENDY COPE (BORN 1945)

British poet Wendy Cope was raised in Kent and her parents often read poetry aloud to her as a child. When her first collection, *Making Cocoa for Kingsley Amis*, was published in 1986, it became a surprise bestseller. She is known for her comic verse, often using humour to address more serious topics.

The Orange, from her 1992 collection, *Serious Concerns*, is about how simple day-to-day things can bring us immense pleasure, especially when we are in love. This poem is loved by many for its delightful simplicity.

At lunchtime I bought a huge orange –
The size of it made us all laugh.
I peeled it and shared it with Robert and Dave –
They got quarters and I had a half.

And that orange it made me so happy,
As ordinary things often do
Just lately. The shopping. A walk in the park
This is peace and contentment. It's new.

The rest of the day was quite easy.
I did all my jobs on my list
And enjoyed them and had some time over.
I love you. I'm glad I exist.

29

Fall, Leaves, Fall

EMILY BRONTË (1818–1848)

Emily Brontë was the English writer best known for her only novel, *Wuthering Heights*. She was the third eldest of the four surviving Brontë siblings and, like her sisters Charlotte and Anne, wrote under a pen name. *Wuthering Heights* – now considered a classic of English literature – was published a year before her death in 1847 and she would sadly never know the fame her novel achieved.

Famously, the Brontës lived in Haworth in Yorkshire, in relative isolation. After the death of their mother, the sisters were sent to the Clergy Daughters' School, where they experienced the harrowing events that were to profoundly affect their writing. Following the deaths of the two older sisters, their father withdrew his daughters, who were then home-schooled by their aunt. Emily, who spent only a brief time at the school, was said to be painfully shy and remains the most elusive of the sisters, leaving almost no personal diaries or letters.

In this poem, Brontë uses visual imagery to describe the sadness and beauty of the passing seasons. Not much is known about the last two years of her life and her faltering health, but this poem is said to be a metaphor for life and death.

Fall, leaves, fall; die, flowers, away;
Lengthen night and shorten day;
Every leaf speaks bliss to me
Fluttering from the autumn tree.

I shall smile when wreaths of snow
Blossom where the rose should grow;
I shall sing when night's decay
Ushers in a drearier day.

30

The Crocodile

LEWIS CARROLL (1832–1898)

Renowned Victorian author Lewis Carroll, born Charles Lutwidge Dodgson, is best remembered for his works for children, *Alice's Adventures in Wonderland* and *Through the Looking Glass, and What Alice Found There*. These books have delighted children and adults alike since they were published in 1865 and 1871 respectively.

The Crocodile appears in Chapter Two of *Alice's Adventures in Wonderland* and is recited by Alice by mistake; she meant to recite a common Victorian poem called *Against Idleness and Mischief* by Isaac Watts. She makes the error because the poem shares the same rhyme scheme as Watts' verse, which starts 'How doth the little busy bee . . .'. *The Crocodile* parodies this poem; the crocodile's corresponding virtues are deception and predation.

How doth the little crocodile
Improve his shining tail,
And pour the waters of the Nile
On every golden scale!

How cheerfully he seems to grin,
How neatly spreads his claws,
And welcomes little fishes in,
With gently smiling jaws!

No Man Is an Island

JOHN DONNE (1572–1631)

Great English poet John Donne's poetry was read by only a small circle of admirers, and although he gained fame as a preacher, his work was never published during his lifetime. He is noted for his religious verse, and his work includes sonnets, poetry, elegies and pamphlets.

Donne wrote *No Man Is an Island* as part of his longer prose work *Meditation 17, Devotions Upon Emergent Occasions*, when he was seriously ill in 1623. Hearing the church bell signifying a funeral, he explores the idea that we are all connected, and when someone dies, it diminishes the larger fabric of humanity. It also says that none of us suffers alone and being aware of each other makes us lead better lives. In the wake of Britain's decision to leave the European Union, this poem resonated with many and was quoted across the globe.

No man is an island, entire of itself;
Every man is a piece of the continent,
A part of the main.
If a clod be washed away by the sea,
Europe is the less, as well as if a promontory were.
As well as if a manor of thy friend's or of thine own
     were.
Any man's death diminishes me
Because I am involved in mankind.
And therefore never send to know for whom the bell tolls;
It tolls for thee.

Meeting at Night

ROBERT BROWNING (1812–1889)

Famous English Victorian poet and playwright Robert Browning is remembered mostly for his dramatic monologues and dark humour, and his best-loved work during his lifetime was the narrative poem *The Ring and the Book*, an astonishing 21,000-lines long and published in four volumes.

Meeting at Night originally appeared in *Dramatic Romances and Lyrics* in 1845, under the title *Night and Morning; I. Night; II. Morning.* It was later separated into two poems, *Meeting at Night* and *Parting in Morning*. Browning wrote the love poem during the time he started courting his future wife; Elizabeth Barrett – a union which turned out to be one of the great love stories of the 19th century.

The grey sea and the long black land;
And the yellow half-moon large and low;
And the startled little waves that leap
In fiery ringlets from their sleep,
As I gain the cove with pushing prow,
And quench its speed in the slushy sand.

Then a mile of warm sea-scented beach;
Three fields to cross till a farm appears;
A tap at the pane, the quick sharp scratch
And blue spurt of a lighted match,
And a voice less loud, through its joys and fears,
Than the two hearts beating each to each!

33

Valentine

CAROL ANN DUFFY (BORN 1955)

Scottish poet Carol Ann Duffy is the UK's first female Poet Laureate. She started writing poetry as a child and was first published aged fifteen. She writes poetry, plays and critical works and tackles difficult subjects, often taking a feminist approach.

Valentine is from a collection of poems entitled *Mean Time*, published in 1993 and written after Duffy was asked by a radio producer to write an original poem for Valentine's Day. In *Valentine*, she explains how an onion is a more powerful gift than flowers or chocolates, and the onion becomes an extended metaphor for love itself.

Not a red rose or a satin heart.

I give you an onion.
It is a moon wrapped in brown paper.
It promises light
like the careful undressing of love.

Here.
It will blind you with tears
like a lover.
It will make your reflection
a wobbling photo of grief.

I am trying to be truthful.

Not a cute card or a kissogram.

I give you an onion.
Its fierce kiss will stay on your lips,
possessive and faithful
as we are,
for as long as we are.

Take it.
Its platinum loops shrink to a wedding-ring,
if you like.
Lethal.
Its scent will cling to your fingers,
cling to your knife.

34

The Little Dancers

LAURENCE BINYON (1869–1943)

Laurence Binyon was a well-respected British poet, dramatist and art scholar. He worked for the Red Cross during World War I as a medical orderly, and one of his best-known works, *For the Fallen*, is often cited on Remembrance Sunday. The fourth verse of this poem has gained an existence of its own, as *The Ode of Remembrance*, with the final words: 'At the going down of the sun and in the morning/We will remember them.'

The Little Dancers takes on a cheerier tone and sums up children's enjoyment at simple pleasures. This poem is a reminder that we can all make our own happiness, whatever the circumstances.

Lonely, save for a few faint stars, the sky
Dreams; and lonely, below, the little street
Into its gloom retires, secluded and shy.
Scarcely the dumb roar enters this soft retreat;
And all is dark, save where come flooding rays
From a tavern-window; there, to the brisk measure
Of an organ that down in an alley merrily plays,
Two children, all alone and no one by,
Holding their tattered frocks, thro' an airy maze
Of motion lightly threaded with nimble feet
Dance sedately; face to face they gaze,
Their eyes shining, grave with a perfect pleasure.

The Night Has a Thousand Eyes

FRANCIS WILLIAM BOURDILLON (1852–1921)

Francis William Bourdillon, a British poet and translator, published a large number of poems in his lifetime but none has endured as much as this one. *The Night Has a Thousand Eyes* has been included in anthologies throughout the years and is loved for its simplicity and ability to convey an idea in just a few simple lines. The poem – containing the message that our entire lives depend on love – is thought to be one of the most enduring love poems of the late 19th century.

The night has a thousand eyes,
And the day but one;
Yet the light of the bright world dies
With the dying sun.

The mind has a thousand eyes,
And the heart but one:
Yet the light of a whole life dies
When love is done.

36

On His Blindness

JOHN MILTON (1608–1674)

John Milton, who was also a historian, pamphleteer and writer of prose, is seen as the most significant British author in history after William Shakespeare. This Petrarchan sonnet, a lyric poem with fourteen lines, was written in 1654, eleven years after Milton's eyesight began to fail. By 1652, he was totally blind but, interestingly, he wrote his most famous works *Paradise Lost* and *Paradise Regained* – considered to be the greatest epic poems in English – after he lost his vision.

Audiences at this time were used to unpicking dense and complex texts, and much of Milton's work revolves around God's relationship with mankind. In this poem Milton meditates on his own loss of sight and fears that his blindness will prevent him from doing God's work. A personified Patience tells him that he is still useful to God, if he continues to have faith.

When I consider how my light is spent,
Ere half my days, in this dark world and wide,
And that one talent which is death to hide,
Lodged with me useless, though my soul more bent
To serve therewith my Maker, and present
My true account, lest he returning chide,
Doth God exact day-labour, light denied?
I fondly ask; but Patience to prevent
That murmur, soon replies: God doth not need
Either man's work or his own gifts, who best
Bear his mild yoke, they serve him best, his state
Is kingly. Thousands at his bidding speed
And post o'er land and ocean without rest:
They also serve who only stand and wait.

37

Silver

WALTER DE LA MARE (1873–1956)

Walter de la Mare was an English poet and novelist who was particularly interested in the imagination of children. He believed that 'children are, in short, visionaries'. *Silver* was first published in 1913 in *Peacock Pie*, a collection of poems for children that is now considered a 20th-century classic.

Silver can be enjoyed for its simplicity of diction and rhyme, giving the perfect snapshot of a clear moonlit night.

Slowly, silently, now the moon
Walks the night in her silver shoon;
This way, and that, she peers, and sees
Silver fruit upon silver trees;
One by one the casements catch
Her beams beneath the silvery thatch;
Couched in his kennel, like a log,
With paws of silver sleeps the dog;
From their shadowy cote the white breasts peep
Of doves in a silver-feathered sleep;
A harvest mouse goes scampering by,
With silver claws, and a silver eye;
And moveless fish in the water gleam,
By silver reeds in a silver stream.

38

there will always be your heart

YRSA DALEY-WARD (BORN 1989)

British author, former model, feminist and poet Yrsa Daley-Ward draws from her own experiences as well as issues affecting today's society. She says: 'I think poetry writing connects with the reader really succinctly – with whatever feeling, whatever emotion. That's what draws me to it, because you can make that connection in a very short amount of space and time.'

Born to a Jamaican mother and Nigerian father, she was raised by her devout Seventh-day Adventist grandparents in the small Lancashire town of Chorley. Her collection of stories *On Snakes and Other Stories* was published in 2013. Originally published through Amazon's self-publishing arm, her debut poetry collection *Bone* was published more widely last year by Penguin Books.

Do not shout for silence
do not shout too loud
there will always be birds outside
a closed
window
a car door shutting in the next
street
fine raindrops,
whispers
footsteps in puddles
some couple somewhere
having an argument
he's telling her to shut up
she's crying
threatening to leave
he's saying he doesn't give a fuck.

Do not shout for silence
do not shout too loud
there will always be
loose change spilled on a
pavement
a plastic bag dancing somewhere
in the
wind,
a tree stretching when it thinks no
one is
there.

There will always be everything
that you
mean but do not say
when I ask you what I've done to
make you so
angry
and the look you give me when
I've
said too much in front of our
friends.

Do not go too far for peace and
quiet
do not run too far
because the country can be as
loud as the city
too noisy in its stillness
and anyway,
there will always be your breath
which, hard as you try,
you can't do without
you can't run away from.
There will always be your heart
beating
stronger and louder
the harder, the further
you run.

Friendship

ELIZABETH JENNINGS (1926–2001)

The work of Elizabeth Jennings, one of Britain's most popular poets of the 20th century, is known for its imagery, emotional sensitivity and logic. She was part of a collective of poets, known as 'The Movement', which included Philip Larkin, Kingsley Amis and Thom Gunn, whose work revealed a shared love of simplicity and regular rhyme and meter.

Jennings published more than twenty books of poetry. In this poem, she describes the fluid and complex psychology of friendship.

Such love I cannot analyse;
It does not rest in lips or eyes,
Neither in kisses nor caress.
Partly, I know, it's gentleness

And understanding in one word
Or in brief letters. It's preserved
By trust and by respect and awe.
These are the words I'm feeling for.

Two people, yes, two lasting friends.
The giving comes, the taking ends
There is no measure for such things.
For this all Nature slows and sings.

40

Thaw

EDWARD THOMAS (1878–1917)

Edward Thomas, a British essayist, novelist and writer, has been labelled 'the master of the short poem'. He wrote all his poetry in a flurry of creativity between 1914 and his death three years later, when he was killed in action at the Battle of Arras during World War I. Most of his poems were published posthumously. He is often considered a war poet, but much of his poetry does not look at the war, and many argue that his work defies classification.

Thomas is known for his observation of the countryside, and this four-line lyric explores how nature is more sensitive to the passing seasons than man.

Over the land freckled with snow half-thawed
The speculating rooks at their nests cawed
And saw from elm-tops, delicate as flower of grass,
What we below could not see, Winter pass.

She Walks in...

LORD BYRON

41

She Walks in Beauty

LORD BYRON (1788–1824)

Lord Byron, born George Gordon, inherited his official title aged ten when his great-uncle died. A flamboyant character who was described as 'mad, bad and dangerous to know', he captured the imagination of Europe. Most of his works, which include the famous *Don Juan*, were said to be inspired by his travels and his Grand Tour of Europe.

Arguably one of the most romantic poems in English literature, *She Walks in Beauty* is often recited during proposals and at weddings. Written in 1814, there has been much speculation about the identity of the woman in the poem. Byron was a notorious womaniser, and some say this poem is an ode to his half-sister Augusta Leigh, with whom he embarked on an affair. Others have said that after meeting Anne Beatrix Wilmot, the wife of his cousin, he was so struck by her beauty that he went home and composed this. The poem celebrates female beauty and the speaker describes both the woman's extraordinary external beauty and inner grace.

She walks in beauty, like the night
Of cloudless climes and starry skies;
And all that's best of dark and bright
Meet in her aspect and her eyes;
Thus mellowed to that tender light
Which heaven to gaudy day denies.

One shade the more, one ray the less,
Had half impaired the nameless grace
Which waves in every raven tress,
Or softly lightens o'er her face;
Where thoughts serenely sweet express,
How pure, how dear their dwelling-place.

And on that cheek, and o'er that brow,
So soft, so calm, yet eloquent,
The smiles that win, the tints that glow,
But tell of days in goodness spent,
A mind at peace with all below,
A heart whose love is innocent!

42

Morning Song

SYLVIA PLATH (1932–1963)

American poet, novelist and short-story writer Sylvia Plath is best known for her semi-autobiographical novel, *The Bell Jar*, and her confessional poetry. She suffered from depression and died by suicide, later becoming one of the most admired poets of the 20th century. In 1982, she became the first person to win a posthumous Pulitzer prize.

Morning Song was published in 1965 – after her death – as part of *Ariel*, a collection of deeply emotive and personal poems. It is said to be a tribute to her daughter, Frieda, who was eight months old at the time of writing in 1961. It describes the arrival of her first baby, and the raw emotions of a new mother in the first few days of a baby's life.

Love set you going like a fat gold watch.
The midwife slapped your footsoles, and your bald cry
Took its place among the elements.

Our voices echo, magnifying your arrival. New statue.
In a drafty museum, your nakedness
Shadows our safety. We stand round blankly as walls.

I'm no more your mother
Than the cloud that distills a mirror to reflect its own
    slow
Effacement at the wind's hand.

All night your moth-breath
Flickers among the flat pink roses. I wake to listen:
A far sea moves in my ear.

One cry, and I stumble from bed, cow-heavy and floral
In my Victorian nightgown.
Your mouth opens clean as a cat's. The window square

Whitens and swallows its dull stars. And now you try
Your handful of notes;
The clear vowels rise like balloons.

43

Bright Star

JOHN KEATS (1795–1821)

The great Romantic poet John Keats is said to have had the most remarkable career of any young English poet. He wrote sonnets, odes, hymns, romances, epics and ballads, and reportedly penned his greatest works between 1818 and 1820, before dying tragically early from tuberculosis, aged just 25.

Bright Star is assumed to be about his beloved Fanny Brawne, whom he met in 1818 and who later became his fiancée, although it is unknown exactly when he wrote it; in some versions, it has the title *Sonnet 1819*. This vivid and melancholy verse expresses the raw emotions of a lover, using powerful imagery where the speaker wishes to be like a star, most likely the North Star. Contrasting beauty and transience, and remoteness and warmth, it exposes his yearning for perfect love and hints at his own impending death.

Bright star, would I were steadfast as thou art —
Not in lone splendour hung aloft the night
And watching, with eternal lids apart,
Like nature's patient, sleepless Eremite,
The moving waters at their priest-like task
Of pure ablution round earth's human shores,
Or gazing on the new soft-fallen mask
Of snow upon the mountains and the moors —
No — yet still steadfast, still unchangeable,
Pillowed upon my fair love's ripening breast,
To feel for ever its soft fall and swell,
Awake for ever in a sweet unrest,
Still, still to hear her tender-taken breath,
And so live ever — or else swoon to death.

44

Sic Vita

HENRY KING (1592–1669)

Henry King was an English poet and Anglican bishop, whose elegy for his wife *The Exequy*, is thought to be one of the finest in the English language.

Sic Vita, or 'Such is Life', alludes to life's brevity in the grand scheme of the universe. The poem suggests that even when we are at our brightest, the moment is borrowed. The message is clear: appreciate your life and the time you have.

Like to the falling of a star;
Or as the flights of eagles are;
Or like the fresh spring's gaudy hue;
Or silver drops of morning dew;
Or like a wind that chafes the flood;
Or bubbles which on water stood;
Even such is man, whose borrowed light
Is straight called in, and paid to night.

The wind blows out; the bubble dies;
The spring entombed in autumn lies;
The dew dries up; the star is shot;
The flight is past; and man forgot.

45

The Best Thing in the World

ELIZABETH BARRETT BROWNING (1806–1861)

Elizabeth Barrett Browning is one of the most accomplished and beloved poets of the 19th century and the Romantic movement, admired for her courage and independence. Her work covered multiple subjects around love, politics and religion. She campaigned for the abolition of slavery, and her work helped to inform child labour legislation reform. Her best-remembered works include *How Do I Love Thee? (Sonnet 43)* and her epic novel *Aurora Leigh*.

This lyrical and playful poem was written in 1855, when Barrett Browning was enjoying married life to Robert Browning, and being a mother. Published posthumously in 1862, the poem reflects on the many beautiful aspects of life and nature, suggesting that there are too many wonderful things in life to pick the best one.

What's the best thing in the world?
June-rose, by May-dew impearled;
Sweet south-wind, that means no rain;
Truth, not cruel to a friend;
Pleasure, not in haste to end;
Beauty, not self-decked and curled
Till its pride is over-plain;
Light, that never makes you wink;
Memory, that gives no pain;
Love, when, so you're loved again.
What's the best thing in the world?
– Something out of it, I think.

46

The Noble Nature

BEN JONSON (1572–1637)

Ben Jonson was an accomplished poet as well as a dramatist, actor and literary critic, and his fame has rested mainly on his satirical dramas, which include *Every Man in His Humour, Volpone; Or, The Fox, The Alchemist* and *Bartholomew Fair*. He is generally regarded as the second-most important dramatist after William Shakespeare during the reign of James VI and I and, at the time, was considered to be as popular. He is often identified as England's first Poet Laureate.

In *The Noble Nature*, Jonson explores what makes man noble, comparing man to a solid oak tree and a delicate lily flower. He suggests that even though a man's life can be short, like the flower, it can be perfect.

It is not growing like a tree
In bulk, doth make Man better be;
Or standing long an oak, three hundred year,
To fall a log at last, dry, bald, and sere;
A lily of a day
Is fairer far in May,
Although it fall and die that night –
It was the plant and flower of Light
In small proportions we just beauties see;
And in short measures life may perfect be.

47

All or Nothing

LANG LEAV (BORN 1983)

The New Zealand-based poet Lang Leav first started writing poems on Tumblr in 2013, where she quickly gained recognition for her musings on feminism, love, loss and self-awareness. Soon she was an international bestselling writer, sitting alongside the other most renowned Instapoets, such as Rupi Kaur. This poem is from her debut poetry collection, *Love & Misadventure*.

If you love me
for what you see,
only your eyes would be
in love with me.

If you love me
for what you've heard,
then you would love me
for my words.

If you love
my heart and mind,
then you will love me,
for all that I'm.

But if you don't love
my every flaw,
then you mustn't love me –
not at all.

48

The Oxen

THOMAS HARDY (1840–1928)

Thomas Hardy is considered to be one of the most masterful novelists of the 19th century, his most famous works including *Far from the Madding Crowd*, *Jude the Obscure* and *Tess of the D'Urbervilles*, but after writing novels he returned to his first love, poetry.

Published on Christmas Eve in 1915 in *The Times*, *The Oxen* is often cited as one of the best Christmas poems in literature. Written by Thomas Hardy during World War I when he was aged seventy-five, it speaks of a yearning for childhood beliefs that the adult speaker no longer has. The idea that the animals in the stable of the Nativity paid homage to Jesus – a notion that is said to be West Country legend – had clearly stuck with him, long after he had stopped having any formal religious beliefs himself.

Christmas Eve, and twelve of the clock.
'Now they are all on their knees,'
An elder said as we sat in a flock
By the embers in hearthside ease.

We pictured the meek mild creatures where
They dwelt in their strawy pen;
Nor did it occur to one of us there
To doubt they were kneeling then.

So fair a fancy few would weave
In these years! Yet, I feel,
If someone said on Christmas Eve,
'Come; see the oxen kneel,

'In the lonely barton by yonder coomb
Our childhood used to know,'
I should go with him in the gloom,
Hoping it might be so.

49

Still, I Rise

MAYA ANGELOU (1928–2014)

American playwright, author, historian, producer, director, performer and civil-rights activist Maya Angelou is best known for her seven autobiographical novels, which include *I Know Why the Caged Bird Sings*.

Still, I Rise was published in her third volume of poetry in 1978, *And Still I Rise*. The poems – which include another of her favourites, *Phenomenal Woman* – focus on an optimistic hope to rise above problems and hardship. She won numerous awards and was awarded over fifty honorary degrees. In 2010, she was awarded the Presidential Medal of Freedom by President Barack Obama, the highest civilian honour in the US.

This empowering poem focuses on Angelou's struggle to overcome injustice and prejudice because of her race. During an interview in 1997, she said that the poem sustained her when times were tough and that people of all races used it in this way.

You may write me down in history
With your bitter, twisted lies,
You may trod me in the very dirt
But still, like dust, I'll rise.

Does my sassiness upset you?
Why are you beset with gloom?
'Cause I walk like I've got oil wells
Pumping in my living room.

Just like moons and like suns,
With the certainty of tides,
Just like hopes springing high,
Still I'll rise.

Did you want to see me broken?
Bowed head and lowered eyes?
Shoulders falling down like teardrops,
Weakened by my soulful cries?

Does my haughtiness offend you?
Don't you take it awful hard
'Cause I laugh like I've got gold mines
Diggin' in my own backyard.

You may shoot me with your words,
You may cut me with your eyes,
You may kill me with your hatefulness,
But still, like air, I'll rise.

Does my sexiness upset you?
Does it come as a surprise
That I dance like I've got diamonds
At the meeting of my thighs?

Out of the huts of history's shame
I rise
Up from a past that's rooted in pain
I rise
I'm a black ocean, leaping and wide,
Welling and swelling I bear in the tide.

Leaving behind nights of terror and fear
I rise
Into a daybreak that's wondrously clear
I rise
Bringing the gifts that my ancestors gave,
I am the dream and the hope of the slave.
I rise
I rise
I rise.

50

Envy

ADELAIDE ANNE PROCTER (1825–1864)

An English poet and philanthropist, Adelaide Anne Procter published her work in Charles Dickens' periodicals, *All the Year Round* and *Household Words* under the pseudonym Miss Berwick. She was actively involved with feminist groups and worked on behalf of unemployed women and the homeless, arguing for equality in education, employment and property rights. She was believed to be the favourite poet of Queen Victoria, and her poems were set to music and made into hymns, but few modern critics have given her work attention.

Envy was written in 1861 and personifies the emotion of Envy, seen as a man who is lucky and whose life is rosy, while the speaker exists in his shadow.

He was the first always: Fortune
Shone bright in his face.
I fought for years; with no effort
He conquered the place:
We ran; my feet were all bleeding,
But he won the race.

Spite of his many successes
Men loved him the same;
My one pale ray of good fortune
Met scoffing and blame.
When we erred, they gave him pity,
But me – only shame.

My home was still in the shadow,
His lay in the sun:
I longed in vain: what he asked for
It straightway was done.
Once I staked all my heart's treasure,
We played – and he won.

Yes; and just now I have seen him,
Cold, smiling, and blest,
Laid in his coffin. God help me!
While he is at rest,
I am cursed still to live: – even
Death loved him the best.

51

Pleasant Sounds

JOHN CLARE (1793–1864)

John Clare is sometimes called the 'peasant poet' because he was the son of an illiterate farmer and became a casual labourer, doing whatever work he could find to make a living. He suffered from delusions and spent the last twenty-five years of his life in a lunatic asylum.

As a poet, he became known for his writing about the English countryside, and his sadness at its decline. His work is often overlooked in accounts of Romantic poetry, but his writing shows a real eye for local detail – as seen in this poem, which is packed with visual imagery.

The rustling of leaves under the feet in woods and under
    hedges;
The crumpling of cat-ice and snow down wood-rides,
    narrow lanes, and every street causeway;
Rustling through a wood or rather rushing, while the
    wind halloos in the oak-toop like thunder;
The rustle of birds' wings startled from their nests or
    flying unseen into the bushes;
The whizzing of larger birds overhead in a wood, such
    as crows, puddocks, buzzards;
The trample of robins and woodlarks on the brown
    leaves, and the patter of squirrels on the green moss;
The fall of an acorn on the ground, the pattering of
    nuts on the hazel branches as they fall from ripeness;
The flirt of the groundlark's wing from the stubbles –
    how sweet such pictures on dewy mornings, when the
    dew flashes from its brown feathers!

52

Everyone Sang

SIEGFRIED SASSOON (1886–1967)

British patriot and poet Siegfried Sassoon is recognised as one of the Great War Poets, whose brutally satirical anti-war poetry brought him critical and popular acclaim. He served in the trenches during the war and was decorated for his bravery.

Everyone Sang was written shortly after the signing of the Armistice treaty on 11 November 1918, which ended World War I. The poem concentrates on the sound of music and voices, and the joy of release from the horrors of the war.

Everyone suddenly burst out singing;
And I was filled with such delight
As prisoned birds must find in freedom,
Winging wildly across the white
Orchards and dark-green fields; on – on – and out of
    sight.

Everyone's voice was suddenly lifted;
And beauty came like the setting sun:
My heart was shaken with tears; and horror
Drifted away . . . O, but Everyone
Was a bird; and the song was wordless; the singing will
    never be done.

Acknowledgements

As Shakespeare said in Twelfth Night: 'I can no other answer make, but, thanks, and thanks and ever thanks. . . .'

To: Liz Gough, Tamsin English, Lauren Whelan, Natalie Bradley, Rosie Stephen, Sally Somers at Yellow Kite; Rachel Kelly; Rowan Lawton and the team at Furniss Lawton; Rory Scarfe; Beth Dufour; and to Chris, Arabella and Alice.

Credits, Copyright and Permissions

The editor gratefully acknowledges permission to reprint copyright material in this collection as follows below:

1. Emily Dickinson, "Hope" is the Thing with Feathers', from Poems by Emily Dickinson, 1891.
2. Rumi, 'The Guest House' from Rumi Selected Poems, translated by Coleman Banks with John Moyne, A.J Arberry and Reynold Nicholson, Penguin Books, 1995. Reproduced with permission from Coleman Barks.
3. D. H. Lawrence, 'Piano', 1918.
4. E. E. Cummings, 'I Carry Your Heart with Me', from Complete Poems: 1904-1962 by E. E. Cummings, edited by George J. Firmage. Copyright 1923, 1951, © 1991 by the Trustees for the E. E. Cummings Trust. Copyright © 1976 by George James Firmage. Used by permission of Liveright Publishing Corporation.
5. Langston Hughes , 'Dreams' from The Collected Poems of Langston Hughes by Langston Hughes, edited by Arnold Rampersad with David Roessel, Associate Editor, copyright © 1994 by the Estate of Langston Hughes. Used by permission from David Higham Associates Ltd and from Alfred A. Knopf, an imprint of the Knopf Doubleday Publishing Group, a division of Penguin Random House LLC. All rights reserved.
6. Edward Lear, 'There Was an Old Man with a Beard' from The Book of Nonsense, 1846.
7. Oscar Wilde, 'In the Forest' from The Lady's Pictorial, 1889.
8. Thomas Campion, 'Now Winters Night Enlarge' from Third and Fourth Books of Ayres, 1617.
9. Edgar Allan Poe, 'A Dream within a Dream', 1849.
10. William Wordsworth, 'Upon Westminster Bridge', from Poems, in Two Volumes in 1807
11. W. H. Davies, 'Leisure' from Songs of Joy and Others, 1911.
12. Walter D. Wintle, 'Thinking' from Unity, Unity Tract Society, Unity School of Christianity, 1905.
13. Alfred Tennyson, 'The Eagle', 1851.
14. W. B. Yeats, 'He Wishes for the Cloths of Heaven' from The Wind Among the Reeds, 1899.
15. Mary Oliver, 'Wild Geese' from Dream Work, Grove/Atlantic, 1986. Used by permission of Grove/Atlantic, Inc.
16. William Blake, 'Infant Joy' from Songs of Innocence, 1789.
17. W. E. Henley, 'Invictus' from The Book of Verses, 1888.
18. Joyce Kilmer, 'Trees' from Poetry: A Magazine in Verse, 1914.
19. Christina Rossetti, 'Echo', 1854 from Goblin Market and Other Poems, 1862.
20. Matsuo Basho, 'The Old Pond' from Matsuo Basho: The Narrow Road to the Deep North and Other Travel Sketches, translated by Nobuyuki Yuasa, Penguin Classics, 1966. Reproduced with permission from The Agency (London) Ltd.
21. Walter Scott., 'Proud Maisie' from The Heart of Mid-Lothian (The Waverley Novels), 1818.

22. Thomas Dekker, 'Cradle Song' from Patient Grissel, Henry Chettle and William Haughton, 1603.
23. William Shakespeare, Sonnet 116.
24. Nikita Gill, 'Temporary and Permanent'. Reproduced with permission from Nikita Gill.
25. Robert Louis Stevenson, 'My Shadow', 1885.
26. Rabindranath Tagore, 'Where the Mind is Without Fear' from Gitanjali (Song Offerings) by Rabindranath Tagore: Gitanjali, 1913.
27. Henry Wadsworth Longfellow, 'The Tide Rises, the Tide Falls', 1880.
28. Wendy Cope, 'The Orange' from Wendy Cope: Serious Concerns, Faber & Faber, 1992. Reproduced with permission from Faber and Faber Ltd and from United Agents.
29. Emily Brontë, 'Fall, Leaves, Fall' from The Complete Poems of Emily Bronte, 1910.
30. Lewis Carroll, 'The Crocodile' from Alice's Adventures in Wonderland, Macmillan & Co Ltd, 1866.
31. John Donne, 'No Man Is an Island', from Devotions Upon Emergent Occasions, 1624.
32. Robert Browning, 'Meeting at Night' from Dramatic Romances and Lyrics, 1845
33. Carol Ann Duffy, 'Valentine' from Love Poems, Picador, 2010. Reproduced with permission from Carol Ann Duffy and Rogers, Coleridge & White Ltd.
34. Laurence Binyon, 'The Little Dancers', ca.1914.
35. Francis William Bourdillon, 'The Night Has a Thousand Eyes', 1899.
36. John Milton, 'On His Blindness', 1655.
37. Walter de la Mare, 'Silver', 1913. Reproduced with permission from the Estate of Walter de la Mare and the Society of Authors.
38. Yrsa Daley-Ward, 'there will always be your heart' from BONE copyright © 2014, 2017 by Yrsa Daley-Ward. Used by permission of Penguin Books Ltd., and from Penguin Books, an imprint of Penguin Publishing Group, a division of Penguin Random House LLC. All rights reserved.
39. Elizabeth Jennings, 'Friendship' from Elizabeth Jennings: New Collected Poems, edited by Michael Schmidt, Carcanet Press, 2002. Used by permission of David Higham Associates Ltd
40. Edward Thomas, 'Thaw'.
41. Lord Byron, 'She Walks in Beauty', 1813.
42. Sylvia Plath, 'Morning Song', from The Collected Poems by Sylvia Plath. Reproduced with permission from HarperCollins Publishers and Faber and Faber Ltd.
43. John Keats, 'Bright Star', 1819 from The Plymouth and Devonport Weekly Journal, 1838.
44. Henry King, 'Sic Vita', 1600s.
45. Elizabeth Barrett Browning, 'The Best Thing in the World', 1885. Reproduced with permission from The Provost & Fellows of Eton College.
46. Ben Jonson, 'The Noble Nature', 1600s.
47. Lang Leav. 'Love & Misadventure', Copyright © 2013 by Lang Leav. Reproduced with permission from Lang Leav and Andrews McMeels.
48. Thomas Hardy, 'The Oxen' from Collected Poems, 1930.
49. Maya Angelou, 'Still I Rise', from And Still I Rise: A Book Of Poems. Copyright © 1978 by Maya Angelou. Used by permission of Virago and of Random House, an imprint and division of Penguin Random House LLC. All rights reserved.
50. Adelaide Anne Proctor, 'Envy' from Legends and Lyrics, 1858.
51. John Clare, 'Pleasant Sounds', 1820s.
52. Siegfried Sassoon, 'Everyone Sang', 1920. Reproduced with permission from the Estate of Siegfried Sassoon and Barbara Levy Literary Agency.